# What's in the Garden?

By Marianne Berkes ❧ Illustrated by Cris Arbo

Dawn Publications

For Emily, who loves to garden, and Libby, who loves to cook. And with fond memories of my years at The Sunshine School in Pawling, New York, preparing nutritious snacks with "kids" many of whom now enjoy healthy eating with their children. — M.B.

To all the teachers, staff, and students in Buckingham County. You all are great! — CA

### Acknowledgments

Thanks to students and Margaret Sims, teacher and master gardener at Palmetto Elementary School for taking Marianne through their bountiful school garden! Thanks also to nutritionists Pat Dugan and Heather Sollohub, who reviewed the recipes. Thanks to Bill Moretz at ProCamera in Charlottesville, Virginia, for photographing the artwork.

Copyright © 2013 Marianne Berkes

Illustrations copyright © 2013 Cris Arbo

### Library of Congress Cataloging-in-Publication Data

Berkes, Marianne Collins.
 What's in the garden? / by Marianne Berkes ; illustrated by Cris Arbo. -- 1st ed.
   p. cm.
 Summary: "Guess what vegetable or fruit this is, growing in the garden! Learn more about it, plus how to eat it in a simple recipe"-- Provided by publisher.
 ISBN 978-1-58469-189-1 (hardback) -- ISBN 978-1-58469-190-7 (pbk.)  1. Vegetable gardening--Juvenile literature. 2.  Kitchen gardens--Juvenile literature. 3.  Cooking (Vegetables)--Juvenile literature.  I. Arbo, Cris, ill. II. Title. III. Title: What is in the garden?
 SB324.B47 2013
 635--dc23

              2012024245

Design and computer production by Patty Arnold, *Menagerie Design & Publishing*
Manufactured by Regent Publishing Services, Hong Kong
Printed January, 2013, in ShenZhen, Guangdong, China

10 9 8 7 6 5 4 3 2 1

First Edition

## Dawn Publications

12402 Bitney Springs Road
Nevada City, CA 95959
530-274-7775
nature@dawnpub.com

Delicious, nutritious, what could it be?
In spring there are blossoms all over the tree.
Red, green, or yellow, with fruit that is round.
If you don't pick it, it plops to the ground.

# APPLE

## Applesauce

8 apples

1 cup water

A pinch of salt

Honey or brown sugar to taste.

Cinnamon to taste

Wash and core apples. Cut into quarters and place in saucepan. Add water and salt. Cook until tender and then mash and put through strainer. Return to saucepan. Add brown sugar or honey to taste and simmer for about three minutes, stirring constantly. Cool and enjoy!

You plant them in rows and each forms a head.
Or else you can grow the "leaf" kind instead.
It grows rather quickly in loose, moist soil,
And if there's some frost, it won't even spoil.

# LETTUCE

## Mixed "Green" Salad

2 handfuls iceberg lettuce

2 handfuls leaf lettuce

2 handfuls spinach leaves

10 or more grape tomatoes

Salt and pepper to taste

2 Tbsp. olive oil

1 tsp. fresh lemon juice

1 tsp. yellow mustard

1 tsp. honey

Rinse salad greens. Pat dry on paper towels. Tear the leaves into smaller pieces and combine in a large bowl, adding rinsed grape tomatoes. For dressing, combine last four ingredients in a jar with a lid and shake. Add dressing when ready to serve so salad does not get soggy. Add salt and pepper to taste.

The part that you eat is way in the ground,
    So how can this fabulous food be found?
Look for the feathery leaves on its top.
    It's long and its orange—a real healthy crop.

## Carrot Muffins

2 cups all-purpose flour

1 Tbsp. baking powder

2 tsp. baking soda

1 tsp. salt

1 tsp. cinnamon

4 large eggs

1 cup applesauce

¼ cup vegetable oil

¾ cup brown sugar

4 cups grated carrots (about 4 large)

Preheat oven to 350°F. Sift together first five ingredients in bowl. In a larger bowl combine eggs, oil, applesauce and brown sugar. Beat well and add flour mixture until moistened. Fold in grated carrots. Spoon into greased muffin pan or use paper liners. Bake 20-30 minutes until lightly browned. Makes about 20. Best with cream cheese frosting!

Its pretty green head is a lovely bouquet
    That sometimes is eaten an interesting way.
Try it uncooked—it's great with a dip—
    Munching the flowery buds on its tip.

# BROCCOLI

## Broccoli Trees

Broccoli

1 8-oz. pkg. of cream cheese

1 8-oz. carton plain yogurt

1 envelope (0.4 oz) dry Ranch salad dressing mix

Place broccoli on cutting board. With small, sharp knife, ask a grown-up to trim off ends of stems to make "spears" with florets. Place in colander under cold running water and rinse. Drain well and serve with dip. For dip, put the cream cheese, yogurt and ranch dressing mix in a medium mixing bowl. Beat with an electric mixer on medium speed until smooth. Refrigerate until ready to use. Makes about two cups.

It's round. It's tiny. It grows on a bush.
When made into sauce, it turns to a mush.
This fabulous fruit can be used as a dye,
And is really yummy in muffins and pie.

# BLUEBERRY

## Libby's Blueberry Pie

2 refrigerated pie crusts (store-bought)

4 cups fresh blueberries (rinsed)

½ cup all-purpose flour

¾ cup sugar

1 Tbsp. fresh lemon juice

1/8 tsp. salt

Preheat oven to 350 degrees. Press one of the pie crusts into 10 inch pie plate. Place blueberries in a large bowl and add flour. Toss to coat. Add sugar, lemon and salt, mixing lightly.

Pour berries into pie shell. Cut other pie crust into 1 inch strips and place on top of crust in criss-cross pattern to form a lattice. Bake 45-60 minutes or until bubbly.

It comes in a bunch and has quite a crunch!
It's chopped up in salad and stew.
But spreading some cream cheese in one of the stalks
Is another fun thing you can do.

# CELERY

## Ants on a Log

Celery stalks

Pkg. of cream cheese

Tub of cottage cheese

Jar of peanut butter

Box of raisins

Rinse celery stalks and dry with paper towels. Put stalks on cutting board and ask a grownup to trim leafy parts off celery stalks with a small sharp knife. With table knife, fill groove of each celery stalk with the spread of your choice. Put a few raisins on top of spread. With peanut butter especially, raisins looks like "ants on a log!"

You eat it in sauces with many a dish,
Or right off the vine—however you wish!
This versatile fruit is even a drink.
Or is it a vegetable? What do you think?

## Easy Tomato Sauce

1 pound of fresh tomatoes

1 Tbsp. olive oil

1 small chopped onion

1 clove garlic, chopped
(or use garlic press)

½ tsp. salt

¼ tsp. fresh pepper

3 tsp. balsamic or sherry vinegar

Fresh chopped basil (optional)

Wash, core and cut tomatoes in half. Put olive oil in baking pan, add tomatoes, and cook in preheated 350°F oven until skins split. Put into a blender and liquefy. Combine remaining six ingredients and simmer on top of stove for 20 minutes. Great on spaghetti and lots of other dishes.

It grows on a vine with skin that is green.
It's sliced in a salad; it's long and it's lean.
But sometimes it's shorter with soft little prickles
And placed in a jar for real tasty pickles.

## Sweet & Sour Cucumber Salad

2 large cucumbers
1 small onion
Salt and pepper to taste
¼ cup vinegar
1 tsp. sugar
¼ cup vegetable oil
¼ cup fresh chopped parsley

Peel cucumbers and slice paper thin. Also slice a small onion into onion rings. Place in serving bowl with cucumbers. Add salt and pepper and toss. Mix the remaining ingredients in a jar or cup with a whisk and pour over cucumbers and onions. Stir and let chill for at least two hours before you serve it.

Just bite its long leaf—you'll be able to tell
The bulb underneath has a very strong smell.
It makes people cry so it's cut in great haste,
But added in cooking, enhances the taste!

# ~ONION~

## French Onion Soup

1 tablespoon butter

1 cup sliced onions

½ tsp. all-purpose flour

½ tsp. sugar

3 cups beef or vegetable broth

1 Tbsp. Worcestershire sauce

3 Tbsp. grated Parmesan cheese

Thick French bread, toasted

Melt butter in large pot. Add onions and slowly cook onions until soft. Stir in flour and sugar and cook one minute. Add broth and Worcestershire sauce. Simmer 30 minutes. Cool and put in refrigerator until ready to serve. Reheat on stove or in microwave. Put one slice of toasted French bread in each serving bowl. Sprinkle with cheese and add reheated soup.

It's usually brown, way down in the soil.
        You scrub it to bake it, or peel it to boil.
It doesn't have ears, but does have eyes—
        It's really a favorite when mashed or as "fries."

# POTATO

## Garlic Mashed Potatoes

4 cups peeled potatoes

1 garlic clove, peeled and halved

1/4 cup warm milk

1/4 cup sour cream

1 Tbsp. fresh parsley, finely chopped

1 tsp. butter or margarine

½ tsp. salt

Pepper to taste

Cut potatoes into quarters. Put potatoes and garlic in a large pot and cover with water. Put a lid on the pot and bring to a boil over medium-high heat. When water begins to boil, remove lid and boil for 20 minutes or until tender when poked with a fork. Drain well and return to pot. Add remaining ingredients and mash until light and fluffy. Makes 4-5 servings.

It has a long ear, but never an eye.
This towering veggie can grow very high.
The kernels are ripened by rays from the sun.
To eat it with butter is really great fun.

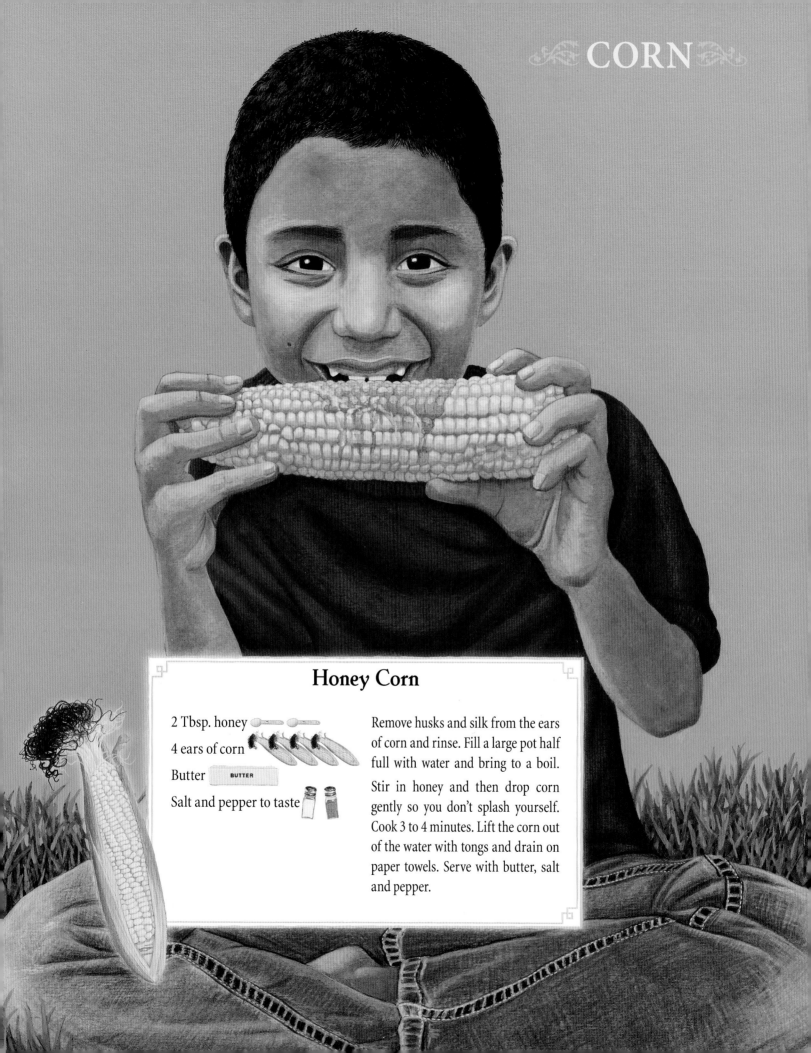

## Honey Corn

2 Tbsp. honey

4 ears of corn

Butter — BUTTER

Salt and pepper to taste

Remove husks and silk from the ears of corn and rinse. Fill a large pot half full with water and bring to a boil.

Stir in honey and then drop corn gently so you don't splash yourself. Cook 3 to 4 minutes. Lift the corn out of the water with tongs and drain on paper towels. Serve with butter, salt and pepper.

It grows in a field, right near the corn.
Frost tops its head on a chill autumn morn.
It's orange and round with a vine that is green,
And kids come to pick it on each Halloween.

# ❦ PUMPKIN ❦

## Roasted Pumpkin Seeds

Pumpkin Seeds

Paper towels

Aluminum foil

Butter or Cooking Spray — BUTTER

Salt or cinnamon and sugar

Preheat oven to 300°F. Wash pumpkin seeds, removing the pulp, and dry them on paper towels. Line a cookie sheet with aluminum foil. Spread a little butter or put cooking spray on the foil and add the pumpkin seeds, arranging them in a thin layer. Sprinkle with sea salt, or with your favorite spices. Bake in oven 30-40 minutes, stirring occasionally, until crisp and golden brown. Remove the shells and enjoy!

Nutritious food for you and me—
        Picked off a vine, or from a tree,
Above the ground, or deep below!
        Isn't it fun to watch it grow?

And when it's ripe and good to eat,
        Why not make a special treat?
Try the recipes in this book,
        And with a grownup start to cook!

# Food For Thought

**Apples** have been around for thousands of years. Colonists brought apple seeds to America. Apple trees like warm summers and cold winters. Did you know that if you cut an apple through the center (crosswise), you will see a star holding brown seeds? Apples are so good for you that there's a famous old saying: "an apple a day keeps the doctor away."

**Lettuce** grows best in cool weather and in rich, well-drained soil. It is low in calories yet high in nutrition, especially lettuce varieties with darker leaves. Want something extra nutritious? Add some spinach leaves to your lettuce salad. Spinach is rich in iron and other minerals. Did you know that lettuce is the second most popular fresh vegetable in the U.S.? (Potato is number one!)

**Carrot** seeds, which are very tiny, grow best in a sunny area in loose, sandy soil where they can easily grow way down into the ground. Almost every known mineral and vitamin is packed into this buried treasure. Thousands of years ago, carrots weren't orange. They were purple and yellow!

**Broccoli** is a rich source of Vitamin C. Usually boiled or steamed, the tips can also be eaten raw. Derived from the Latin word brachium which means "branch," broccoli has been a favorite with Italians since the Roman Empire. Take a close look and you will see lots of branches with groups of heads, called "florets," almost ready to flower.

**Blueberries** were a favorite fruit of Native Americans, who also used the juice to dye fabrics and baskets. They are ready to harvest when the green-pink berries turn dark blue. This sweet juicy fruit contains healthy fibers, minerals, vitamins and antioxidants. Because there is a star-shaped formation on the berry left over from the flower, it was originally called a "star berry."

**Celery** originated in the Mediterranean area and has long been used as a medicine and a spice, as well as a food. Celery seeds and dried celery leaves are used for flavoring. But celery is most popular for its long U-shaped stem with a great crunchy texture. Celery is loaded with nutrients.

**Tomatoes** were first cultivated in ancient Mexico, the word coming from the Aztec *tomatl*, meaning "swelling fruit." Technically a tomato is a fruit, but because it is not sweet like most fruits, it is treated like a vegetable. An excellent source of vitamins and minerals, tomatoes are eaten many different ways and widely grown around the world.

**Cucumbers** originated in India, and are one of the oldest known cultivated foods. The plant is a creeping vine that is often grown on a trellis to take up less space and keep the fruit from rotting on the ground. Sliced cucumbers are refreshingly crunchy with about 90 percent water. Pickles are cucumbers marinated in salty water, often with spices, for a week or more.

**Onions** thrive best in direct sunlight and fertile soil. The word comes from the Latin *unio* meaning one, because it grows from a single bulb. When cut, onions make people cry because cutting them releases sulfur into the air. Even so, onions are very popular, especially when cooked with other food. Can you name three colors of onions sold in grocery stores? (Red, white and yellow.)

**Potatoes** are underground "tubers" that grow from the plant stems. The plant itself is poisonous, but the tuber (unless it is green) is safe to eat and is a wonderful source of nutrition and energy. Potatoes first grew in the high mountains of South America. Sailors brought them to the rest of the world in the late 1500's. There are thousands of varieties!

**Corn** was cultivated thousands of years ago in Mexico and Central America. The native peoples called it *maize*. Corn plants typically grow eight feet high! Corn is eaten in many ways—on the cob, as a cereal, ground into flour, tortillas, or hominy, pressed into oil, made into a sweet syrup or alcohol, or fed to animals for meat. It is even made into a gasoline additive!

**Pumpkins** are often grown near corn since they smother weeds and help corn roots retain moisture. This is known as "companion planting." They are famous as pies, but their seeds taste great when roasted too. When the soft inside of a pumpkin is scooped out, it can be carved into a Jack-o-lantern. Pumpkins can be huge and gain as many as 25 pounds a day. The biggest one on record is over 1000 pounds!

# How Does Your Garden Grow?

## Fruit or Vegetable?
To a scientist, the plant part that contains seeds is called the "fruit." But more commonly, only sweet fruits like apples or blueberries are called fruits, while all other plant parts are considered vegetables. That means that tomatoes and pumpkins, for instance, are both a fruit and a vegetable! There is also one other vegetable in this book that is also a fruit. Can you find it?

## How Do Plants Start?
A "parent plant" usually makes seeds that can grow into a new plant. Seeds are often dispersed to new places by wind or water. Animals also help. A seed might stick to an animal and later drop off. Or an animal might eat a fruit containing seeds, and poop them out far away.

People who plant seeds need to know what kind of soil to plant them in, how far apart to plant them, how deep they should go, and especially the right time to plant. Some plants do better in cooler weather, while others need to be planted after all danger of frost is past. Pumpkins, for example, like warmer weather and can take up to four months to mature. That's important to know—at least if you want them to be ready for Halloween.

## What Plants Need:
- **L**ight and heat, which the sun provides
- **A**ir, from which they take carbon dioxide
- **W**ater, which gives hydrogen and oxygen
- **N**utrients found in the soil
- **S**pace for them to spread out and grow.

(An easy way to remember: It spells the word "LAWNS" going down!)

## Pollinators, Please!
About 75 percent of plants need pollinators to reproduce. The pollinators are usually bees, wasps, moths, butterflies, flies, beetles, birds, and many other animals. Can you find the pollinators illustrated in this book?

# Plant Parts

## Plants Have Six Parts!

1. Roots absorb water and nutrients from the soil.

2. Stems hold up the plant and carry water and minerals.

3. Leaves contain a green pigment called chlorophyll that plants use to trap energy, usually from the sun, to make food. This process is called photosynthesis.

4. Flowers have several parts, including the anther, which has pollen. When insects and birds are attracted to a flower, the pollen sticks to the stigma part of other flowers they visit. This is how pollination happens.

5. Fruits grow if the flower is pollinated, and hold the seeds.

6. Seeds grow into new plants.

&#x273F; Can you name the five plant parts of the pumpkin plant shown above?

&#x273F; Can you name the plant parts of the fruits and vegetables in this book?

&#x273F; Can you put together a salad using all six plant parts?

&#x273F; What kinds of pies could you make from the fruits in this book?

# Let's Get Cookin'

## Reap What You Sow

Do you have a garden at your home or school? I've visited some schools where kids are growing gardens in their school yards, and learning healthy eating habits too! At harvest time, vegetables are used in school cafeterias for students to enjoy. As the old proverb goes, it's fun to "reap what you sow."

So let's get cookin'! You will learn what goes into a dish as you make healthy choices about the food you eat. It can also help you read, do math and organize things. Here are some important basics before you begin.

&#x273F; Read the recipe with a grown up to see if it is something you would like to try together.

&#x273F; Gather the cooking tools you will need (measuring cups and spoons, bowls, cutting board, baking pans, aprons, oven mitts, etc.)

&#x273F; Review the list of ingredients and get them ready.

* Read the recipe instructions carefully, making sure you follow the steps in the right order.
* Always rinse fresh fruits and vegetables under cold water. Some of them may need preparation before you start cooking, i.e. slicing, peeling, grating.

## Words to Cook With

* Bake – cooking food in an oven
* Beat – stirring quickly until smooth
* Boil – when a liquid reaches the boiling point it is very hot and "bubbles."
* Colander – a strainer that allows liquid to drain through while solids stay inside
* Core – removing the core (hard central part) of a fruit
* Cream – beating soft butter and sugar to a creamy consistency
* Fold – adding ingredients gently to retain air in the mixture
* Garlic press – a kitchen utensil to crush garlic cloves through a grid of small holes
* Grate – rubbing food against a grater to make coarse shreds
* Mash – crushing food to a smooth texture
* Preheat – heating the oven to the correct temperature before you begin
* Sift – to pass flour, etc. through a sieve or flour sifter
* Simmer – cooking over a low heat so the liquid or food is not boiling
* Tbsp. – Abbreviation for tablespoon
* Toast – browning or crisping food in a toaster or in the oven
* Tongs – grasping devices with long handles
* Tsp. – abbreviation for teaspoon
* Whisk – a gadget that evenly mixes things together

## Garden Songs, Books and Websites

"Dirt Made My Lunch" by the Banana Slug String Band includes the song "Roots, Stems, Leaves," http://www.songsforteaching.com/bananaslugstringband/rootsstemsleaves.htm

*A Seed is Sleepy* by Dianna Hutts Aston, (Chronicle Books, 2007)

*First Garden: The White House Garden and How it Grew* by Robbin Gourly (Clarion, 2011)

*Gardening with Children* (BBG Guides for a Greener Planet), (Brooklyn Botanic Garden, 2011)

*Healthy Foods from Healthy Soils* by Elizabeth Patten and Kathy Lyons (Tilbury House Publishers, 2003)

*How to Grow a School Garden*, a Complete Guide for Parents and Teachers (Timber Press, 2010)

*Roots, Shoots, Buckets & Boots: Gardening Together with Children* by Sharon Lovejoy (Workman, 1999)

http://urbanext.illinois.edu/firstgarden/

http://www.choosemyplate.gov/

http://www.jmgkids.us/

www.edibleschoolyard.org

www.kidsgardening.org

http://www.enchantedlearning.com/subjects/plants/

Many more free teaching and learning ideas from Marianne are available, such as "Supermarket Botany" and "An Apple A Day." Go to www.dawnpub.com, select "Teachers/Librarians," then "Downloadable Activities." You can also download the twelve recipes and reproducible book marks.

MARIANNE BERKES HAS SPENT MUCH OF HER LIFE as a teacher, children's theater director and children's librarian. She knows how much children enjoy "interactive" stories and is the author of many entertaining and educational picture books that make a child's learning relevant. Reading, music, theater, gardening, and cooking have been a constant in Marianne's life. Her books are inspired by her love of nature. Marianne hopes to open kids' eyes to the magic found in our natural world. She now writes full time. An energetic presenter at schools and conferences, Marianne believes that "hands on" learning is fun. Her website is **www.MarianneBerkes.com**.

CRIS ARBO'S ART IS KNOWN FOR INTENSE DETAIL and is inspired by her love and respect for nature. It has appeared in books, magazines, calendars, cards, murals, and in animated feature films, TV shows, and commercials. She has illustrated six nature awareness children's books for Dawn Publications and is also a frequent presenter at schools and conferences. Cris has four daughters and lives in Buckingham, Virginia with her husband, author Joseph Anthony and their youngest daughter, Alina. Many of Cris' favorite hours are spent in the garden.

Photo by Lisi Stoessel

## ❧ALSO BY MARIANNE BERKES❧

*Over in the Ocean: In a Coral Reef* — With unique and outstanding style, this book portrays a vivid community of marine creatures. **This book is also available as an app-an animated,interactive game!**

*Over in the Jungle: A Rainforest Rhyme* — As with "Ocean," this book captures a rain forest teeming with remarkable animals.

*Over in the Arctic: Where the Cold Winds Blow* — Another charming counting rhyme introducing creatures of the tundra.

*Over in Australia: Amazing Animals Down Under* — Australian animals are often unique, many with pouches for the babies. Such fun!

*Over in the Forest: Come and Take a Peek* — Follow the tracks of ten woodland animals but . . . uh-oh . . . watch out for the skunk!

*Seashells by the Seashore* — Kids discover, identify, and count twelve beautiful shells to give Grandma.

*Going Around the Sun: Some Planetary Fun* — Earth is part of a fascinating "family" of planets. Here's a glimpse of the "neighborhood."

*Going Home: The Mystery of Animal Migration* —This winning combination of verse, factual language, and beautiful illustrations is a solid introduction to animals that migrate.

## ❧ALSO ILLUSTRATED BY CRIS ARBO❧

*The Dandelion Seed* — A fitting symbol of life filled with challenge, wonder, and beauty.

*In a Nutshell* — The tale of an acorn is a tale about life.

*In the Trees, Honey Bees* — A marvelous inside-the-hive view and insight into the life of bees.

*All Around Me, I See* — A magical journey of nature, filled with both imagination and reality.

*Earth Heroes: Champions of the Ocean* —The life stories (with an emphasis on their youth) of eight of the world's most influential people in protecting the oceans.

Dawn Publications is dedicated to inspiring in children a deeper understanding and appreciation for all life on Earth. You can browse through our titles, download resources for teachers, and order at www.dawnpub.com or call 800-545-7475.